TOO
GOOD
to be
TRUE

ALSO BY CLIFF CARDINAL

Huff & Stitch

TOO GOOD *to be* TRUE

Cliff Cardinal

Effie,

Don't trust your parents!

Cliff Crd

PLAYWRIGHTS CANADA PRESS
Toronto

Too Good to be True © Copyright 2021 by Cliff Cardinal

No part of this book may be reproduced, downloaded, or used in any form or by any means without the prior written permission of the publisher, except for excerpts in a review or by a license from Access Copyright, www.accesscopyright.ca.

For professional or amateur production rights, please contact:
The GGA
250 The Esplanade, Suite 304, Toronto, ON M5A 1J2
416.928.0299, http://ggagency.ca/apply-for-performance-rights/

LIBRARY AND ARCHIVES CANADA CATALOGUING IN PUBLICATION
Title: Too good to be true / Cliff Cardinal.
Names: Cardinal, Cliff, author.
Description: A play.
Identifiers: Canadiana (print) 20210343346 | Canadiana (ebook) 20210343362
 | ISBN 9780369102904 (softcover) | ISBN 9780369102911 (PDF)
 | ISBN 9780369102928 (HTML)
Classification: LCC PS8605.L5574 T66 2021 | DDC C812/.6—dc23

Playwrights Canada Press operates on land which is the ancestral home of the Anishinaabe Nations (Ojibwe / Chippewa, Odawa, Potawatomi, Algonquin, Saulteaux, Nipissing, and Mississauga), the Wendat, and the members of the Haudenosaunee Confederacy (Mohawk, Oneida, Onondaga, Cayuga, Seneca, and Tuscarora), as well as Metis and Inuit peoples. It always was and always will be Indigenous land.

We acknowledge the financial support of the Canada Council for the Arts, the Ontario Arts Council (OAC), Ontario Creates, and the Government of Canada for our publishing activities.

For Tantoo and Riel.

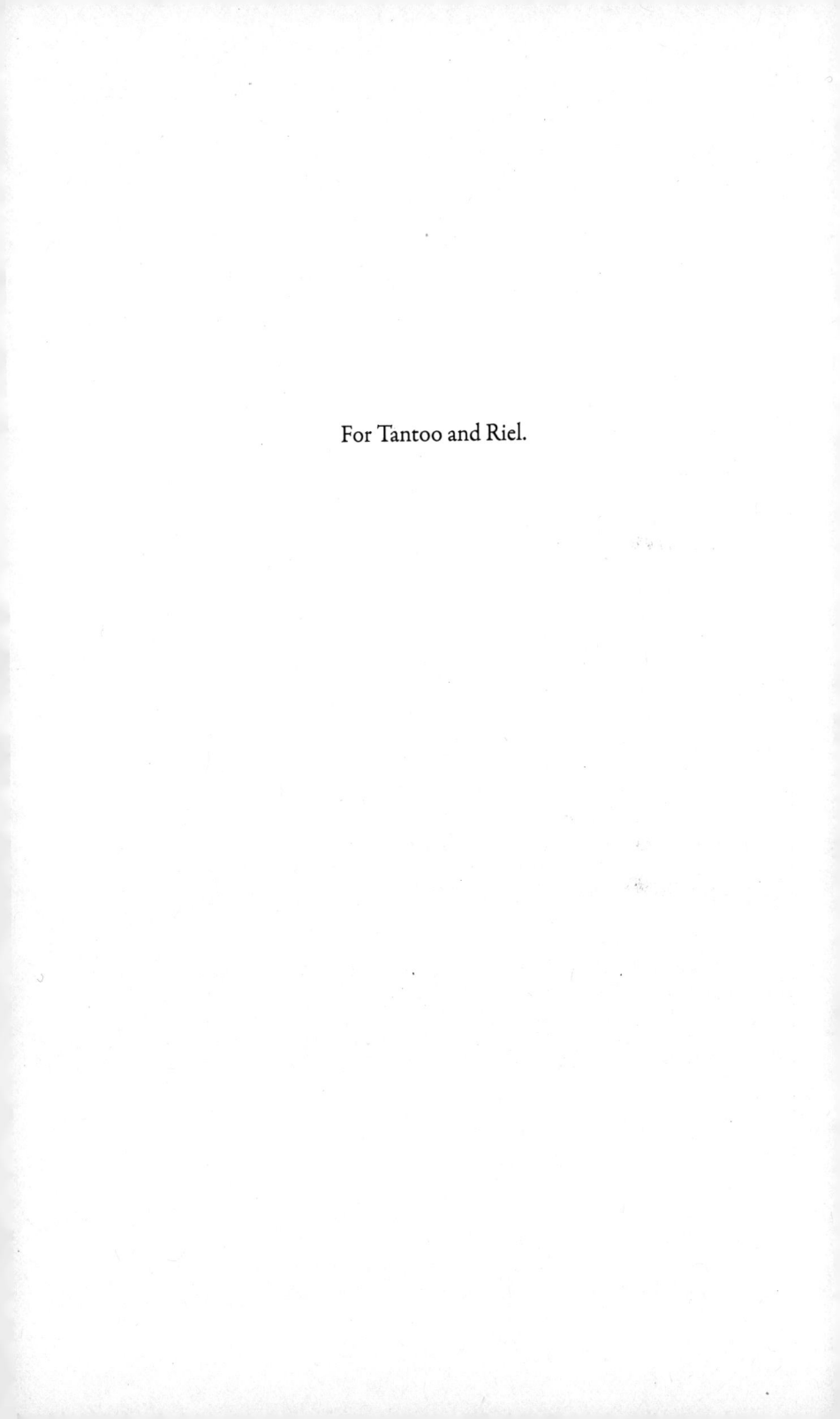

Too Good to be True was first produced by Video Cabaret in Toronto from April 29 to May 19, 2019, with the following cast and creative team:

Maria: Cheri Maracle
Jude: Ryan Cunningham
Lisa: Patti Shaughnessy

Director: Cliff Cardinal
Lighting Design: Andrew Dollar
Costume Design: Sage Paul
Dramaturgy: Brian Drader and Deanne Taylor

CHARACTERS

Maria: thirties, mom to Lisa and Jude.
Lisa: fifteen, daughter to Maria, sister to Jude.
Jude: eleven, son of Maria, brother to Lisa.

PROLOGUE

MARIA: Shh.
Kids, wait there.

LISA: Mom, where are we?

MARIA: Shh.

> *Beat.*

JUDE: What's going on, Mom?

> *Beat.*

MARIA: The realtor said she hid the key under a rock; but you know what, she must have forgot.
I'm gonna have to just...

> *Maria exits.*

> *Glass shatters.*

LISA: Mom.

> *The lock clicks open.*

> *Beat.*

SCENE I: NEW DIGS

MARIA is holding a "For Sale" sign.

MARIA: Come on in, kids.

Beat.

Welcome home.

JUDE: Whoa.
This house is awesome.

Beat.

LISA: Sure is.

Beat.

JUDE: If there's a top bunk, can I have dibs?

Beat.

LISA: Mom, who lives here?

Beat.

MARIA: We do.

Beat.

LISA: We do.

MARIA: We do.

LISA: Whoa, no way.

Beat.

MARIA is carrying as much baggage as she can, and then a little bit more.

MARIA: This is your house, honey.

LISA: Wow.
Mom ... seriously.

MARIA: Seriously.

Beat.

LISA: Well ... whose furniture is this?

Beat.

MARIA: Ours.

Beat.

JUDE: Awesome.

Beat.

MARIA: The house is staged.
The realtor brings in sparse bits of furniture so families can project their own hopes and dreams.

Can you feel the warmth?

LISA: Yeah.
I can.

JUDE: We're like those families on *Home Makeover*.

> *Beat.*

MARIA: Yeah.

> *Beat.*

JUDE: Where their house is broken, but the production company shows up and gives them an amazing new house that they didn't really earn, but you feel like they deserve anyway.

> *Beat.*

MARIA: Our house is not broken.

JUDE: Our house is a van.

> *Beat.*

LISA: Mom, we really live here.

MARIA: Yes.

> *Beat.*

I mean the paperwork isn't finished yet.

> *Beat.*

But we live here now.

Beat.

JUDE: The fridge has a built-in icemaker.

LISA: When till the paperwork is done?

JUDE: The coffee maker has a frothing wand.

LISA: When till the mortgage is paid?

JUDE: There's a bathroom.

Beat.

LISA: When— There is?

Beat.

MARIA: Nothing too good for my kids.

Beat.

LISA: But how can we afford this?

Beat.

MARIA: I didn't want you to find out like this.

MARIA rolls her shoulders.

Thunder and lightning.

But houses are inexpensive if a horrific tragedy occurs inside.

Beat.

Like if an entire family is stabbed to death as they sleep.

Beat.

Or if they commit mass suicide by imbibing a mixture of cyanide, tranquilizers and Kool-Aid.

Beat.

Or even if somebody leaves the gas stove on and everybody asphyxiates face down in steaming bowls of oatmeal.

LISA: But hmm...

Beat.

MARIA: It's terrible when that happens.

Beat.

But the upside is: these houses become very affordable.

LISA: But hmm...

JUDE touches his penis.

MARIA: Do you have to pee?

Beat.

JUDE: No.

MARIA: Then stop touching your penis.

JUDE: I'm not touching my penis.

Beat.

Oh, yeah.

Beat.

LISA: So, if we live here, is he going back to school?

MARIA: Yes.

Beat.

Eventually.

Beat.

LISA: If he doesn't go to school, everyone will think we're inbred.

Beat.

JUDE: How come only I have to go to school?
How come she doesn't have to go back to school?

Beat.

MARIA: Your sister's gonna have a full-time job as a mom.

Beat.

And also she must take time to find healing.

Beat.

Honey, after what you've been through, you can't expect to—

LISA: So you're going to home-school him.

MARIA: Yes.

Beat.

Home-school.
Home-school on the fly.

Beat.

LISA: Is there an official paper you're supposed to get?

MARIA: We don't need some paper that shows how smart we are.

JUDE: Colleges might.

Beat.

MARIA: Haven't you been learning a lot.

Beat.

All that history, at those national monuments.
All that math, calculating the miles to the next hotel.

Beat.

I've taught you both how to drive.

Beat.

You wouldn't have learned that in fourth grade.

Beat.

Now, for the first lesson in the great Maria Grace home-school experiment: living every day like it's the last episode of the season.

Beat.

JUDE: Whoa, awesome.
The last episode of the season is where the whole world almost falls apart but then the hero risks it all to save what he cares about most.

Beat.

MARIA: That's right.

Beat.

MARIA: I've still got a few more tricks to show you. Then we'll go back to school.

Beat.

JUDE: I have a question I've been meaning to ask you.

Beat.

MARIA: Let the home-schooling begin.

Beat.

JUDE: What's a fugitive?

Beat.

Beat.

Beat.

MARIA: A fugitive is someone who wants to clear their name.

Beat.

JUDE: That's not what she said.
She said a fugitive is someone who everyone is chasing because they want to know all about you.

    Beat.

LISA: That's celebrities . . . not fugitives.

    Beat.

JUDE: What's the difference between fugitives and celebrities?

    Beat.

MARIA: Public opinion.

    Beat.

JUDE: Hmm . . .

    Beat.

LISA: Mom, I need to know, no kidding: is this our—

MARIA: Yes.
Why do you keep asking me that?

LISA: It just seems . . .
Doesn't it?

JUDE: What?

    Beat.

LISA: A little too good to be true.

Beat.

JUDE: Nope.

Beat.

MARIA: Honey, nothing is too good for you.

Beat.

Now grab the rest of your stuff.

Rock music.

JUDE exits.

LISA exits.

MARIA exits.

Beat.

LISA moves a suitcase into the bedroom, off.

JUDE moves a suitcase into the bedroom, off.

JUDE enters smoking a joint.

Beat.

LISA enters with a box.

JUDE gives the joint to LISA, takes a box and exits.

LISA smokes the joint.

MARIA enters.

LISA gives the joint to MARIA and exits.

MARIA smokes the joint.

JUDE enters with a frilly valise.

MARIA takes the frilly valise, hands JUDE the joint and exits.

JUDE smokes the joint.

The lights fade out.

SCENE II: SCHRÖDINGER

Beat.

LISA: When the baby comes, can we put the crib right here?

Beat.

MARIA: Have you thought about baby names?

LISA: If it's a girl, I was thinking... Jennifer Lopez.

Beat.

MARIA: If he's a boy?

LISA: Um...

Beat.

MARIA: It must be hard to think about, because you were hurt.

Beat.

But you're safe now, honey.
No one's ever gonna touch you again, no ma'am.

LISA: Mom, listen...

MARIA: Yes, honey, yes: I'm listening.

Beat.

Beat.

LISA: Uh . . . never mind.

Beat.

JUDE enters with an empty cat carrier.

LISA: What?

JUDE: I-I . . . I forgot the cat—

Beat.

At the motel.

Beat.

I forgot the cat.

Beat.

LISA: You lost the cat.

Beat.

JUDE: I let her out for some air and this girl started talking to me.

Beat.

MARIA: What girl?

Beat.

JUDE: *(to MARIA)* Then you called...
I forgot to bring her back.

MARIA: Who did you talk to?

LISA: You lost our cat?

JUDE: Oh no oh no oh no...

Beat.

MARIA: Baby, focus.

Beat.

JUDE: Can we go back?

MARIA: No, that motel is—
Did they seem like they knew you?

JUDE: You know, she did.

Beat.

MARIA: Did you tell her your name?

JUDE: I said Jude.
I didn't say my last name.

Beat.

LISA: Idiot.

Beat.

MARIA: What else did you say?

Beat.

JUDE: Just that our old life wasn't fair; so we're looking for a new one. Like you said.

Beat.

MARIA: Like I said...
I said "don't talk to anyone."

Beat.

Remember.
Don't talk to anyone.
Don't talk in front of anyone.
And if someone talks to you first—

JUDE: Tell them I don't speak English.

Beat.

LISA: You weeping colon.

JUDE: Wart sucker.

LISA: Facial cyst.

JUDE: Goat molester.

LISA: Sexual deviant.

JUDE: Depraved swine.

LISA: Dingleberry.

JUDE: Scabie.

LISA: Glue sniffer.

JUDE: Oozing pustule.

LISA: Future pedophile.

Beat.

MARIA: Enough now; he knows what he's done. You can't make him feel worse.

LISA: I can make him feel worse.

Beat.

You're adopted.

JUDE: You smell cat's a—

MARIA: I didn't want you to find out like this.

MARIA rolls her shoulders.

Thunder and lightning.

LISA: / Huh. /

JUDE: / Find out what. /

Beat.

MARIA: You're adopted.

Beat.

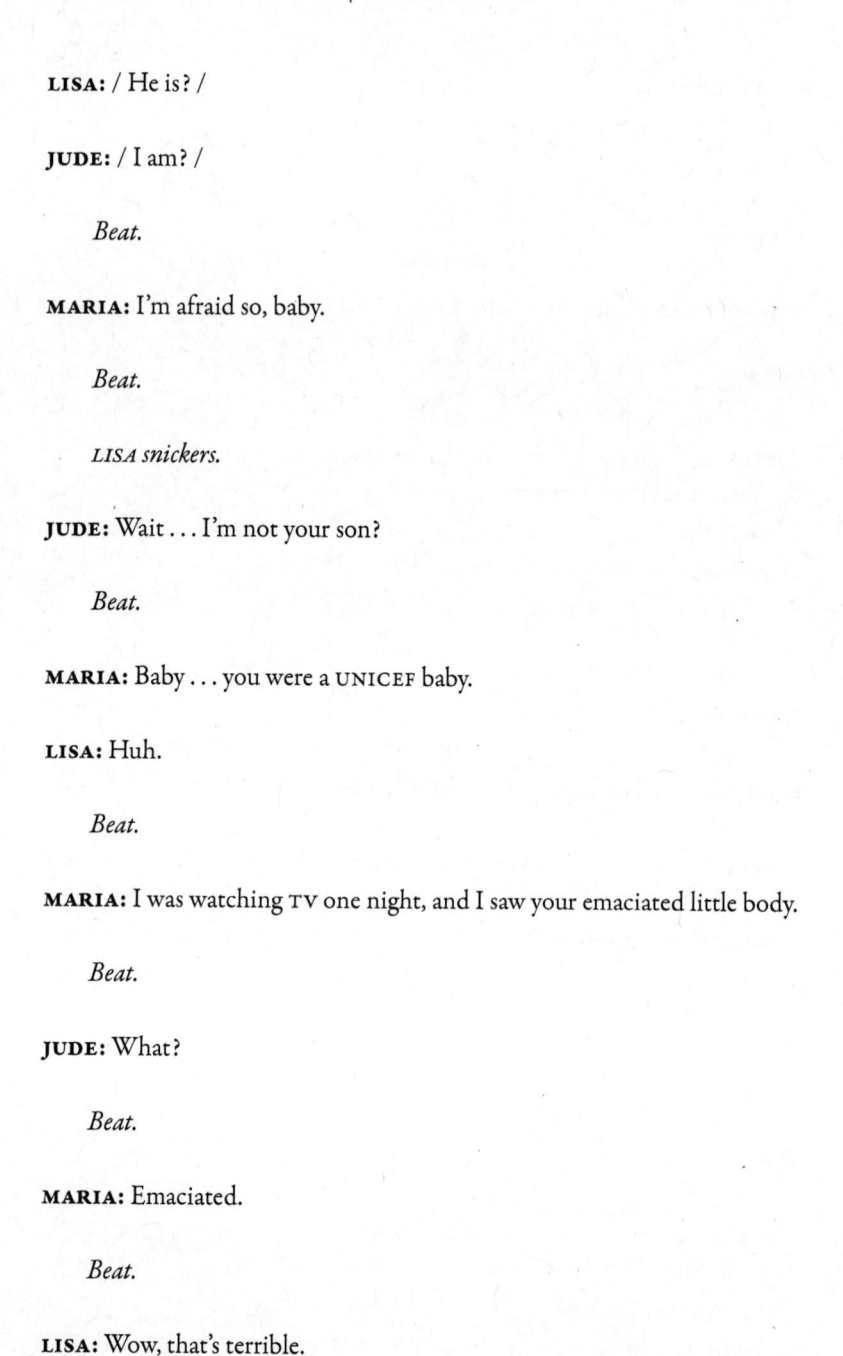

LISA: / He is? /

JUDE: / I am? /

Beat.

MARIA: I'm afraid so, baby.

Beat.

LISA snickers.

JUDE: Wait... I'm not your son?

Beat.

MARIA: Baby... you were a UNICEF baby.

LISA: Huh.

Beat.

MARIA: I was watching TV one night, and I saw your emaciated little body.

Beat.

JUDE: What?

Beat.

MARIA: Emaciated.

Beat.

LISA: Wow, that's terrible.

JUDE: Wow, that's total bull—

MARIA: Sure is.

Beat.

Then I found out . . . that . . . they sell these kids.

Beat.

Once you turned three, they'd've sold you to rebels . . . who'd've conditioned you into a child soldier.

Beat.

LISA: Amazing story, Mom.

Beat.

MARIA: I did what any compassionate human being would do: I stole you.

Beat.

I wrapped you up and carried you away.

Beat.

LISA: How'd you get him past the customs agent?

Beat.

MARIA: Great question, honey.
I blew him.

Beat.

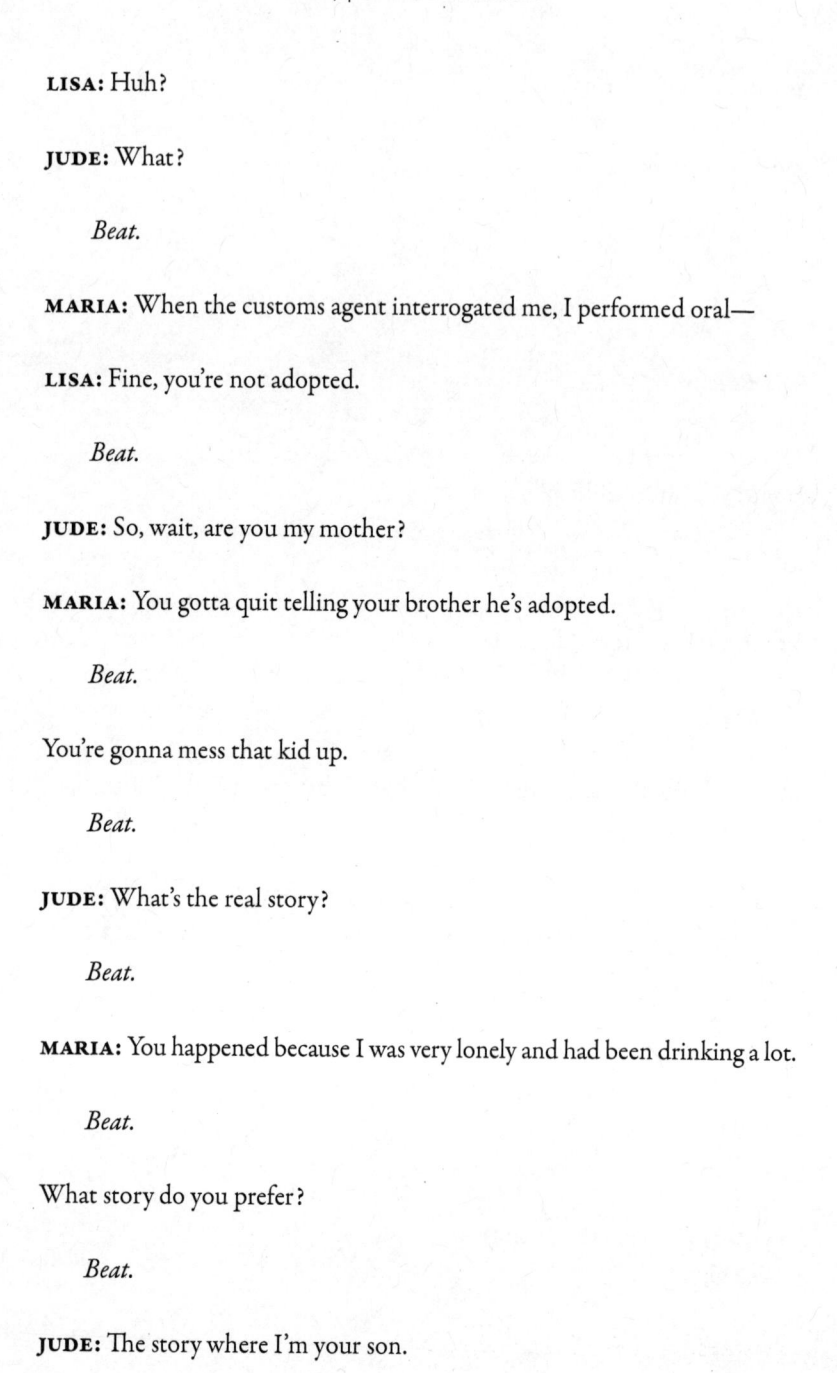

LISA: Huh?

JUDE: What?

Beat.

MARIA: When the customs agent interrogated me, I performed oral—

LISA: Fine, you're not adopted.

Beat.

JUDE: So, wait, are you my mother?

MARIA: You gotta quit telling your brother he's adopted.

Beat.

You're gonna mess that kid up.

Beat.

JUDE: What's the real story?

Beat.

MARIA: You happened because I was very lonely and had been drinking a lot.

Beat.

What story do you prefer?

Beat.

JUDE: The story where I'm your son.

Beat.

No: African war child.

JUDE exits.

Beat.

MARIA: I hope you learned something today.

Beat.

LISA: Like what?

Beat.

How to get through customs.

JUDE returns.

JUDE: *(sees a valise)* Hey, what's in the frilly case?

Beat.

MARIA: Frilly case . . . Stay out of my valise.

Beat.

LISA: What's the big deal?

JUDE: Yeah, what's in the valise?

Beat.

MARIA: Let's just sit down for a second.

Beat.

Here . . . in the . . . solarium.

Beat.

Beat.

One day, when you're older, you're going to better understand your mom; but, in the meantime, there are some things we can never talk about.

Beat.

LISA: You're being weird.

Beat.

MARIA: If you open this valise, if you look inside, you can never unlook inside.
You'll always have seen.
Your mom doesn't want that.
Now I want you both to promise me that, no matter what, you'll never look inside this valise.

Beat.

LISA: Sure.

JUDE nods.

Beat.

MARIA raises her right hand.

MARIA: May my soul burn in the fiery depths of hell if I ever betray my mother.

Beat.

Say it.

Beat.

LISA: / May my burning fiery depthen . . . /

JUDE: / May my soul's burning fire . . . /

Thunder and lightning.

Beat.

MARIA: May my soul burn in the fiery depths of hell if I ever betray my mother.

Beat.

LISA: / May my soul burn in the fiery depths of hell if I ever betray my mother. /

JUDE: / May my soul burn in the fiery depths of hell if I ever betray my mother. /

Beat.

MARIA: Don't look in the frilly valise.

Beat.

LISA: I thought we don't believe in hell.

Beat.

MARIA: We do now . . .

The phone rings.

Beat.

Beat.

(to JUDE*)* No.

JUDE: *(answers the phone)* Grace residence, how may I direct your call?

Beat.

My mom ... she can't come to the phone right now.

Beat.

She's got circus practice.

Beat.

She's an aerialist.
She flies through the air and turns tricks.

Beat.

MARIA: *(mouths)* Hang up.

JUDE: Hang up.

Beat.

MARIA: No, you hang up.

JUDE: No, you hang up.

Beat.

You must be calling for the people who used to live here.
Apparently, there's been a terrible oatmeal tragedy and they're all dead now.

> *Beat.*

> MARIA *hangs up the phone.*

LISA: Mom, you said we—

MARIA: We live here.
It's just the house hasn't been transubstantiated into our name yet.

> *Beat.*

LISA: Oh.

> *Beat.*

> LISA *exits.*

> *Beat.*

> *Rock music.*

> MARIA *hallucinates:*

MARIA: Every night I dream my daughter gives birth to a healthy baby girl.

> LISA *nurses a possum baby.*

> *Beat.*

My son will learn healthy sexual boundaries.

> JUDE *pulls worms from his underwear*

Beat.

Every night I dream my family will be safe.

A bear menaces MARIA.

The lights fade out.

SCENE III: ROUGHHOUSING

LISA: Dear Trevor.

Beat.

Dear Trevor.

Beat.

First of all, I'm sorry about my mom; she can be so embarrassing.

Beat.

Second of all, I forgive you for what you said.
I mean, I guess what I said wasn't much better.

Beat.

I want you to know that . . . if he's a boy . . . I'm gonna name our baby after you.

Beat.

JUDE enters, unseen.

LISA: Sometimes I imagine a world where we end up together.
I'd stay at home in our mansion and take care of our babies and you'd be off scoring touchdowns in the NFL.

Then, on any given Sunday—

JUDE: Um, do you have an imaginary boyfriend?

    Beat.

LISA: He's not imaginary.
He's dead.
Moron.

    Beat.

JUDE: He'd probably rather be dead than be your boyfriend.

LISA: One more word...

    Beat.

...and you eat this vase.

JUDE: Take me with you to the NFL.

LISA: Ugh.

    Beat.

    LISA throws the vase.

    The vase shatters off stage; glass splinters in MARIA's arm.

    MARIA enters, protecting her arm.

MARIA: Oh no oh no oh no.

    Beat.

LISA: What?

MARIA: I've got glass in my arm.

> *Beat.*

> *Beat.*

> *Beat.*

The itsy bitsy spider climbed up the waterspout
Down came the rain and washed the spider out
Out came the sun and dried up all the rain
And the itsy bitsy spider climbed up the spout again

> *Beat.*

LISA: Lemme see.

> *Beat.*

MARIA: No, I just need to think.

LISA: Mom.

> *Beat.*

Lemme see.

> *Beat.*

JUDE: Can we go to the hospital?

> *Beat.*

MARIA: No, we can't go to a hospital.

Beat.

JUDE: Whatever we did, it can't be that bad.

Beat.

Can we please, please, please go to the hospital?

MARIA: / No. /

LISA: / We can't. /

JUDE: Why not?

MARIA: Your mom . . . I did . . . uh, perpetrated, I guess—

LISA: Mom, could you please shut up for a second?

Beat.

(to JUDE) You're gonna be my assistant, okay, buddy?

JUDE nods.

We need sterile bandages, some kind of disinfectant and a pair of needle-nose pliers from the tool kit.

Beat.

JUDE exits.

Beat.

Let's get that glass out of your arm, Mom.

Beat.

Come into the light.

> *Beat.*

> *Beat.*

> *Beat.*

MARIA: How's it look?

LISA: Oh, just great.

> *Beat.*

You've got a few shards of glass sticking out of a . . . tendon.

MARIA: How many?

LISA: Oh let's not get into that.

> *Beat.*

Do you have any pre-existing medical conditions?

> *Beat.*

MARIA: I'll be fine—I'll just wear sleeves.

> *Beat.*

> *Beat.*

> *Beat.*

> *JUDE enters holding needle-nose pliers.*

JUDE: Pliers.

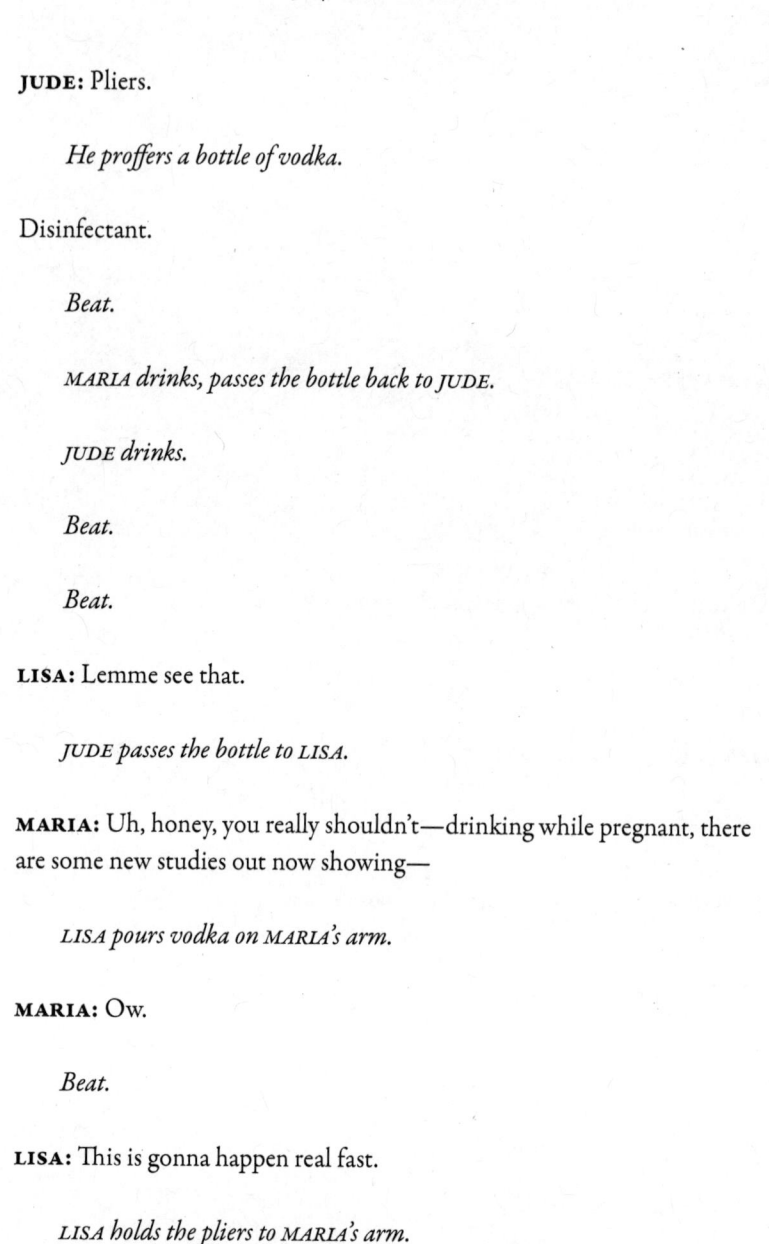

> *He proffers a bottle of vodka.*

Disinfectant.

> *Beat.*

> *MARIA drinks, passes the bottle back to JUDE.*

> *JUDE drinks.*

> *Beat.*

> *Beat.*

LISA: Lemme see that.

> *JUDE passes the bottle to LISA.*

MARIA: Uh, honey, you really shouldn't—drinking while pregnant, there are some new studies out now showing—

> *LISA pours vodka on MARIA's arm.*

MARIA: Ow.

> *Beat.*

LISA: This is gonna happen real fast.

> *LISA holds the pliers to MARIA's arm.*

MARIA: Ow.

Beat.

LISA: I haven't done anything yet.

Beat.

MARIA: Oh.

Beat.

LISA: *(sings)* The itsy bitsy spider climbed up the waterspout—

/ *LISA plucks a shard.* /

MARIA: / Ow. /

/ *JUDE sings along.* /

LISA: Down came the rain and washed the spider out—

/ *She plucks a shard.* /

MARIA: / Ow. /

LISA: Out came the sun and dried up all the rain—

/ *Plucks a shard.* /

MARIA: / Ow. /

LISA: And the itsy bitsy spider . . .

MARIA blacks out.

Beat.

Beat.

Beat.

MARIA is under the effect of a flagging paralytic.

LISA: Scalpel.

JUDE: Scalpel.

LISA: Clamp.

JUDE: Clamp.

LISA: Suction.

JUDE makes a suction sound.

Dropping pressure.

JUDE: We're losing her.

LISA: Clear.

JUDE: Clear.

MARIA is shocked by a defibrillator.

Golf Saturday?

LISA: You betcha.
Close 'er up.

JUDE: Have you seen my watch?

The lights fade out.

Beat.

The lights fade in.

MARIA: Ooohwee.

Beat.

Good.

Beat.

I feel better already.

Beat.

JUDE enters.

JUDE: How'd you know what to do?

Beat.

Beat.

Beat.

LISA: Mom.

Beat.

I'm sorry.

Beat.

MARIA: No.
You performed an emergency medical procedure without going to medical school.
What does that tell you?

LISA: I shouldn't throw vases.

Beat.

MARIA: If you hadn't thrown the vase, you wouldn't know you could perform surgery.

Beat.

LISA: Not sure this is first-rate medical care.

JUDE: Or even first-world medical care.

Beat.

MARIA: We all make mistakes.

JUDE: Kinda makes losing the cat seem not so bad.

Beat.

LISA: *(to JUDE)* You're deplorable.

Beat.

SCENE IV: LISA'S STORY

Beat.

JUDE: Who are we running from?

Beat.

MARIA: The police.

Beat.

JUDE: I thought we were running from the Terminator.

Beat.

MARIA: What happened was . . . your sister got her first boyfriend.

LISA eavesdrops.

He was a couple grades older.

JUDE: Yeah, I remember Trevor.
Quarterback of the football team.

Beat.

That wasn't all it was cracked up to be.

LISA: You don't know anything.

Beat.

We were in love.

Beat.

MARIA: You were.

Beat.

LISA: It was the most enchanting and fulfilling two weeks of my life.

Beat.

We talked.
We laughed.
We had the most intense ...

Beat.

Moments.

Beat.

We were inseparable, meant to be.

Beat.

Like two trains colliding in the night.

Beat.

MARIA: Um, something went wrong though, right?

Beat.

LISA: Huh.

Beat.

Oh yeah.

Beat.

One night, Trevor came to me in the field behind the park.

MARIA: Wait.
I thought you said he came to you after school.

LISA: It was twilight.
Twilight is after school, is it not?

Beat.

One night, after school, at twilight . . .
Trevor came to me in his truck, to the field behind the park, just as we had several times before.
But something was different. He was cold, mean.
He wanted me.
But I said "no."

Beat.

Beat.

Beat.

MARIA: He forced her.

Beat.

Now she's going to be a mom...

Beat.

And Trevor...

Beat.

Let's just say he's not gonna be ready for the playoffs.

Beat.

JUDE: You killed Trevor Murphy?

Beat.

MARIA: *(to LISA)* I didn't know you liked him so much.

Beat.

LISA: I can't do this.
I can't do this.

MARIA: Honey, you can do this.
You are so brave.

Beat.

LISA: No, listen: I'm not brave.

MARIA: *(to JUDE)* Can you think of anyone braver?

JUDE: The firefighters on 9/11.

Beat.

MARIA: Absolutely, the brave firefighters who made the ultimate sacrifice on 9/11.

Beat.

But—

JUDE: What about the troops?

Beat.

MARIA: Of course, we can't ever forget about the heroic men and women of the armed forces who lay their lives on the line every day to protect our freedom.

Beat.

But aside from them, do we know of anyone braver than—

JUDE: Astronauts.

Beat.

MARIA: Okay, but—

JUDE: Sewer cleaners.

Beat.

MARIA: Yes, you're right, it takes an incredible amount of courage to voyage in space or clean the sewers.

Beat.

JUDE: Rodeo clowns.

Beat.

MARIA: Yep... also a courageous occupation.

Beat.

But can we say: aside from the selfless firefighters on 9/11, the heroic men and women of the armed forces, astronauts, sewer cleaners and rodeo clowns—

Beat.

Your sister is the bravest person we know.

Beat.

JUDE: You're also the most beautiful girl I've ever seen.

Beat.

LISA: Really?

JUDE: I guess I mean that more as a gesture.

Beat.

Music. The baby kicks.

LISA winces.

Beat.

MARIA helps LISA to the couch.

Beat.

JUDE exits.

Beat.

LISA sits on the couch.

Beat.

MARIA exits.

Beat.

Beat.

Beat.

SCENE V: AERIALISM

JUDE enters.

JUDE: Hey, I've been thinking maybe the cat is alive.

Beat.

She could sneak onto the grill of a transport truck and hide next to the fuel tank.

Beat.

Then, maybe, traffic would have to slow down for a terrible accident.

LISA: You're a terrible accident.

Beat.

JUDE: Say a cement truck merges into a family of five and smears their mangled, decapitated bodies against the guardrail.

Beat.

It's terrible when that happens.

Beat.

But then everyone has to slow down to see.

Beat.

With traffic slowed, the cat could scamper down the vines along the freeway overpass and take the path to the bus stop.

Beat.

Then once she's at the bus stop—she could go anywhere.

Beat.

LISA: Hey, come here for a second.
You got something on your face.

Beat.

JUDE: No.

Knock, knock, knock.

MARIA enters.

Knock, knock, knock.

MARIA: Hide.

Beat.

MARIA wields a Swiss Army knife.

Beat.

The knocking ceases.

Beat.

JUDE and LISA emerge.

LISA: You said we lived here.

Beat.

MARIA: I just needed a bit of space to clear my head before the next big push.

LISA: You lied again.

MARIA: It was true for a little while.

LISA: Then you'd make something else up to be true for a little while.

Beat.

MARIA: Then I'd find us something new to believe in.

Beat.

JUDE: You left us at the motel.

Beat.

LISA: For three days.

Beat.

MARIA: I know I'm not perfect.

Beat.

But when I'm with you guys, I've got a perfect life.

Beat.

LISA: We live in a van.

   Beat.

You're a . . . an aerialist.

   Beat.

MARIA: You must be real ashamed, huh.

   Beat.

JUDE: What's to be ashamed of?
Aerialism sounds beautiful.
Flying through the air.
Turning tricks.

   Beat.

Performing private aerial functions at fancy motel convention centres.

   Beat.

LISA: We bathe in truck stop bathrooms.

   Beat.

Other families we see, they're making some big, life-changing move. They're packing up and going somewhere special.

   Beat.

But we're not.

   Beat.

And it's not fair.
It's not fucking fair.

> *Beat.*

MARIA: I think I let you down, kids.

> *Beat.*

I'm just a no-good mom, I guess.

> *Beat.*

I won't get a chance to reinvent myself.
But if you do: make a good self.

> *Beat.*

Okay, if you don't want to come with me, I'll drop you off anywhere you want.

> *Beat.*

LISA: I just wish we were normal.

> *Beat.*

MARIA: Honey, we're not normal.

> *Beat.*

You pulled glass from my arm.

> *Beat.*

A normal person couldn't do that.
We're weirdos.

Beat.

Beautiful weirdos.

Beat.

And we're going somewhere special too.

Beat.

LISA: We're not going anywhere.

SCENE V.D

Rock music: MARIA's stripper song.

MARIA performs a non-sexual lap dance for JUDE.

JUDE giggles.

Beat.

JUDE exits.

MARIA rests on the couch.

The lights fade out.

SCENE VI: THE FRILLY VALISE

Beat.

JUDE enters.

Beat.

JUDE: There's still one thing I don't get.

MARIA: That's okay, baby.
Sometimes we don't have to understand.
We can just let the question wash over us.

Beat.

JUDE: What's in the frilly valise?

MARIA: Stay out of the frilly valise.

Beat.

LISA: What's the big deal, Mom.

JUDE: Yeah, what's the big deal?

Beat.

MARIA: The big deal . . . is . . . uh . . .

MARIA rolls her shoulders.

I didn't want you to find out like this.

JUDE: Uh oh.

Beat.

MARIA: But, it's time.

LISA: Time for what?

MARIA: For supper.

Lightning crashes.

At the last supper, Jesus broke open a piece of matzo.

Beat.

LISA: Jesus.

JUDE: Matzo.

Beat.

MARIA: He said, "Eat this bread, for it is my body."

Beat.

LISA: Huh.

JUDE: I'm bored.

Beat.

MARIA: The next day he went to Jerusalem.

Beat.

I can't remember what happens then.

Beat.

But to this day, Catholics perform the Eucharist.
That means they believe Christ's body literally transforms into the bread and wine.

Beat.

LISA: I thought we don't believe in Jesus.

MARIA: We do now.

Beat.

Lightning and rolling thunder.

The night I killed your boyfriend, something came over me.

Beat.

I lured him to the van.

Beat.

I stabbed him to death and cut up his body with my Swiss Army knife.

Beat.

LISA: Mom, cut the shit.

Thunder and lightning.

MARIA: I kicked the legs, torso and head out of the van.

Beat.

Then I grabbed the arm.

Beat.

I thought killing Trevor would make you whole.
But nothing was different.
I wanted what we could never have: justice.

Beat.

He took your flesh.

LISA: Listen.

MARIA: Now, honey.

LISA: I need to tell you.

MARIA: We're taking it back.

Beat.

LISA: Huh.

Beat.

MARIA: Enjoy your meal, and don't ever forget this supper.

Beat.

LISA: Okay, whatever.

LISA eats.

Mmm... dead boyfriend chili.

Beat.

JUDE eats a spoonful.

Beat.

JUDE: This is good.

MARIA: Whatever's wrong with your mom...

Beat.

I cook a mean chili, right?

Beat.

JUDE: So, what's in the frilly case?

Beat.

LISA: Don't you get it?

Beat.

That's where Mom's supposedly been storing remnants of my boyfriend's decomposing corpse to eventually find a moment, like this one, to cannibalize him in a ceremony of... transubstantiation.

Beat.

MARIA: Supposedly.

Beat.

LISA: Mom, the cops are after us.

Beat.

At some point you have to admit the truth.

MARIA: If I'm lying, look in the valise.

Beat.

LISA: You're obviously lying.

Beat.

MARIA: So look.

Beat.

LISA: I'll look.

Beat.

MARIA: Go ahead.

Beat.

LISA: I will.

Beat.

MARIA: Why aren't you?

Beat.

LISA: Like there's really human flesh in there.

Beat.

MARIA: If there's not, what's the shame in having a peak?

Beat.

LISA: I will.

Beat.

MARIA: So do.

Beat.

LISA looks in the valise.

Beat.

LISA: Oh.

Beat.

Oh.

Beat.

No, don't look.

Beat.

Stay away.

Beat.

Feow.

Beat.

MARIA: Do you feel better?

Beat.

JUDE: I wanna see.

LISA: No . . . the cold, dead flesh would permanently scar your imagination.

Beat.

JUDE: Come on.

LISA: Now spin around in circles and say a hundred times that your soul will burn in the fiery depths of hell if I ever disobey my sister.

Beat.

JUDE exits.

Beat.

Close one.

MARIA: Oh, you have no idea.

Beat.

LISA: Mom, I think you might be a pathological liar.

MARIA: Uh huh.

JUDE sneaks the valise off stage.

LISA: Does it bother you when I say that?

MARIA: Does what bother me?

Beat.

LISA: That you're a pathological liar.

MARIA: No.

LISA: No.

MARIA: Some people are way worse off.

JUDE enters with a massive white dildo.

Ack.

LISA: Ack.

MARIA: Ack.

LISA: Ack.

Beat.

JUDE: Hey, Mom, look:

JUDE holds the base of the dildo to his forehead.

I'm a sexicorn.
Nay nay nay.

Beat.

They laugh and laugh and laugh.

Beat.

Beat.

Beat.

SCENE VII: A DARK SECRET

Beat.

Beat.

Beat.

LISA: I never said no.

Beat.

Beat.

MARIA: Well—

LISA: I said—

MARIA: Did—

LISA: Yes.

Beat.

MARIA: Oh.

Beat.

Beat.

Beat.

Oh.
You . . .
Lisa.

    Beat.

    Beat.

    Beat.

LISA: His friends saw us.

    Beat.

He got embarrassed.

    Beat.

Said I was a fat slut.

    Beat.

I didn't know you would kill him.

    Beat.

    MARIA rolls her shoulders.

    Beat.

    MARIA gives LISA her knife.

MARIA: Here.

Beat.

The three-and-a-half-inch camper is the perfect tool for all your outdoor adventures.
Equipped with two blades, can and bottle openers and a wood saw, this is the ultimate tool for the outdoor enthusiast.
The camper carries a lifetime warranty, stainless steel implements and unsurpassed Swiss-made quality and durability.

Beat.

Available in both red and black.

Beat.

A knock at the door.

JUDE enters.

JUDE: The police are here.

MARIA: Kids, this may be the only moment we ever get, but if we live it hard enough, it'll be the only one we ever need.
Okay . . . be with me.

/ JUDE nods. /

LISA: / Okay, Mom. /

Knock, knock.

MARIA: Kids, go and play under the sink.

Beat.

Beat.

Beat.

Beat.

MARIA leaves the house to confront the police.

Hey, copper.

Beat.

Don't come any closer.
This here in my hand is a detonator.

Beat.

I got this house rigged with enough C4 to blow the whole block to kingdom come.

Beat.

You and your men better fall back until . . .
I figure out what the ox balls I'm gonna do.

MARIA goes back inside.

Beat.

JUDE: Woah, you rigged the house with C4?

Beat.

MARIA: Yeah . . . and I know kung fu.

Beat.

LISA: Kung fu.

The phone rings.

MARIA: Go ahead, baby, show them how nice your phone manners are.

Beat.

JUDE answers the phone.

JUDE: Grace residence, how may I direct your call . . .
(to MARIA) It's for you.

MARIA nods.

May I ask what this is regarding, please?

Beat.

Seems to be about Trevor Murphy's dismembered body.

Beat.

(into the phone) What's that?

Beat.

Trevor Murphy is alive.

Beat.

MARIA: / He is? /

LISA: / He is? /

Beat.

Beat.

JUDE: That is not current, sir.

>Beat.

Sir, you are mistaken: he is quite dead, I ate him myself.

>Beat.

>*JUDE holds the receiver mute to his chest.*

He says Trevor's not dead.

LISA: Find out... has he asked about me?

>Beat.

JUDE: ... You're gonna have to give us a second to process this.

>*JUDE hangs up.*

They musta stitched him back together and reanimated him. Like Frankenstein.

>Beat.

MARIA: I may have fudged some of the facts.

>Beat.

I didn't lure him, exactly.

>Beat.

I was driving home—you were getting so big.

>Beat.

... And there he was: crossing the street with his stupid gym bag.

Beat.

I just ... bumped him.

Beat.

JUDE: Apparently he has awoken from his coma.

Beat.

MARIA: I wish I'd known that before I rigged the house with C4.

Beat.

LISA: Mom, we've got to get you out of here.

Beat.

MARIA: How?

Beat.

LISA rolls her shoulders.

LISA: I feign a seizure.

Beat.

Yeah, pregnant kid with a seizure.

Beat.

The cops will all turn into a bunch of heroes for sure.

While they're strapping me down . . . that's when you jump from the attic to a tree and climb down.

>   *Beat.*

>   *A police helicopter settles over the house.*

>   *Beat.*

>   *Beat.*

>   *Beat.*

MARIA: I think it's the end of the line, kids.

JUDE: Wait, there may be one more thing I can do.

>   *Beat.*

What if you sign over the rights to your story to me?

>   *Beat.*

I've been doing some research, and there's big interest in fugitive stories.

>   *Beat.*

Now, with the whole cannibalism spin . . . we're can't miss.

>   *Beat.*

MARIA: Sell my story.

>   *Beat.*

Make a bunch of money and be famous for telling everyone what a nut job I am.

    Beat.

JUDE: No.

    Beat.

In our story, you're going to be brave and warm and loving... and my hero.

    Beat.

My sister is going to be a good mom... and a hand surgeon.

    Beat.

LISA: *(to MARIA)* You need to have that looked at.

    Beat.

JUDE: And new baby... he's gonna be the baby now.
And I'm gonna be the man.

    Beat.

And we'll take all the money and get a fancy new house.
And a fancy new van.
And a fancy new lawyer.
And we'll always be there for each other no matter what.

    Beat.

You think it'll sell?

Beat.

LISA: Yeah, I think it'll sell.

MARIA dons earrings and heels.

MARIA: If I'd know I was getting arrested, I'd have worn a dress.

MARIA exits.

Beat.

Beat.

Beat.

LISA: Remember that time...

Beat.

JUDE: Yeah.
And you—

LISA: Yeah, and we...

Beat.

JUDE: And Mom goes...

Beat.

LISA: We shoulda...

Beat.

Next time.

>   *Beat.*

JUDE: Next time.

>   *Beat.*

>   *MARIA enters.*

>   *Beat.*

MARIA: Now, now, chins up.
What do I always say?

LISA: I didn't want you to find out like this.

>   *Beat.*

JUDE: Stop touching your penis.

>   *Beat.*

MARIA: Say it with a little sugar.

>   *Beat.*

These past three months have been the privilege of—

>   *LISA's water breaks.*

>   *Beat.*

JUDE: Uh oh.

Beat.

LISA: *(to JUDE)* Get the kid's pool and fill 'er up with warm water. Get some towels from the bathroom, and we're gonna need a pair a scissors.

Beat.

MARIA: No, honey.
You need immediate medical attention.

LISA: Help me get undressed.
We're doing this right here.

Beat.

MARIA: Honey, we can't—

LISA: Mom, move the goddamn coffee table and hold those cops off.

Beat.

Can you get us two more hours?

Beat.

MARIA: I'm sure I can think of something.

MARIA leaves the house.

As the lights fade out, LISA gives directions to JUDE.

MARIA rolls her shoulders.

Blackout.

EPILOGUE

VOICE-OVER: Maria Grace plead guilty to reckless driving causing bodily injury and was sentenced to two years in the Grand Valley Institution for Women.

Lisa is a paramedic living in Kitchener, Ontario, with her daughter, Jennifer Lopez Grace.

Jude's TV show, *Maria Gets a New Life* debuts on Netflix this fall.

End of play.